Hispanic Heritage: Volume 5

The Great Migration: From Farms To Cities

Richard Sanchez

Published by Abdo & Daughters, 4940 Viking Drive, Suite 622, Edina, MN 55435.

Library bound edition distributed by Rockbottom Books, Pentagon Tower, P.O. Box 36036, Minneapolis, Minnesota 55435.

Photos by:
Bettmann Archive: 14, 20, 24, 27
Archive Photos: 6, 12, 15, 16, 23

Edited by John Hamilton

Library of Congress Cataloging–in–Publication Data
Sanchez, Richard, 1954-
    The great migration: from farms to cities / Richard Sanchez
        p.   cm — (Hispanic heritage; v.5)
    Includes bibliographical references (p. 31) and index.
    ISBN 1-56239-335-9 (lib. bdg.). -- ISBN 1-56239-385-5 (pbk.)
    1. Hispanic Americans—Migrations—Juvenile literature.
[1. Hispanic Americans—Migrations.] I. Title. II. Series.
Hispanic heritage (Edina, Minn.); V.5.
E184.S75S266   1994
307.2'4'08968073—dc20   94-23398
                        CIP
                        AC

CONTENTS

1
INTRODUCTION

Hispanic culture in the United States at the start of the 20th Century was very different from what it is today. It was sometimes hard to tell Hispanic culture apart from Anglo culture. It had become popular for Hispanics and Anglos to marry one another. And Hispanics were very interested in looking, talking and acting like Anglos so they could be part of one big happy American family.

However, not all Hispanics liked the idea of melting together with Anglos. They thought the Hispanic traditions and way of life were special. But many unexpected events worked together to make sure Hispanic culture would not disappear in the 20th Century. One of them was the great flow of Hispanics from all over the world into the United States. They brought with them the culture of their native lands and helped keep alive the traditions of their heritage.

Many of these newcomers to the United States were drawn to the farms and ranches of rural America. But later in the century large numbers of them would be attracted to the big cities where jobs in factories and shops awaited.

2
THE FLOW BEGINS

The story of these great movements of people begins at the end of the Spanish American War at the close of the 19th Century. Spain's defeat gave the United States control of Cuba, Puerto Rico and the Philippines. Living conditions were terrible in each of those places. The United States felt it had a responsibility to fix things so democracy could take hold.

The United States also felt it had to do something to help its neighbors throughout Latin America. The nations of Central and South America seemed in such constant misery. It seemed as if all the wealth and power in those nations was in the hands of a fortunate few families while everyone else suffered. There were revolutions, but nothing seemed to get better no matter how much blood was spilled.

Unfortunately, the help offered by the United States did not make much difference. If anything, the situation for many people only grew worse.

Many people decided to pack up and move to the United States. They had heard what life was like in the United States. They knew it as a land where anything and everything was possible. It was a place where poor people could become wealthy. It was a land where people who never were allowed to go to school could still do great things with their lives. The United States was a wonderful country brimming with hope.

Moving to the United States was easy during the first two decades of the 20th Century. There were no laws to keep people from freely entering and living here. (This is called an "open border" policy.) In fact, the United States actually welcomed anyone who was poor, suffering and weak. Not until the 1920s were there any limits on the number of people who could come to the United States.

Factories were a source of jobs for Hispanic immigrants willing to work long hours for little pay.

3
UPHEAVAL IN MEXICO

People from Mexico were very glad the United States had an open-border policy. In 1910 there was a blood-soaked revolution in their country. Tens of thousands of Mexicans flooded across the U.S. border in search of safety.

But many who came to the United States did not know how to take advantage of the good things that awaited them. They could not speak English, the language of the Anglos. Nor did they understand the culture of America. For those reasons many immigrants found themselves trapped in more poverty and more despair.

They also came in search of jobs. The United States had entered a period of massive industrialization. Factories began springing up in the big cities of the Northeast, Midwest, Southeast and Southwest. The companies that owned the factories needed workers. People who took the jobs had to work long hours. Sometimes they worked every day of the week with no days off and no vacations. For all their hard work, the people received very low pay. The pay was even lower in the Southwest. A dollar a day was about all a worker could expect in wages. Few Anglo and European immigrants were willing to work for so little money. But many Hispanics were.

Until this time, most newly arrived Hispanics lived on farms or in rural communities. Most were very poor. Then they began hearing the stories of factory owners in the cities who were looking for workers. They were told the pay wasn't much. But that didn't matter. These Hispanics were so poor that the little money offered by the factory owners seemed like a lot by comparison. And so they moved to the cities.

When they arrived, they found themselves forced to live in the poorest neighborhoods. They called these poverty zones "los barrios."

Workers of all kinds were treated badly in those days. It wasn't long before they began fighting back against the factory owners. They tried to organize unions in order to get higher pay and better working conditions.

But the factory owners didn't want that to happen. They hired thugs to beat up and sometimes kill workers who wanted to belong to the unions.

Hispanics faced much discrimination from employers in the United States. Because Hispanics were willing to work for so little money, people got the idea it was okay to cheat them of a fair wage. And to make matters worse, many of the new immigrant Hispanics could not speak English well enough to argue for what was right.

There arose in the big cities efforts among Hispanics to gain political power. They studied the Constitution and learned how the American system of government works. They realized they could make the system work for themselves. But to do so meant getting Hispanics to vote for Hispanics or for people who would help pass laws benefitting Hispanics.

4
A BETTER LIFE

Many Hispanics in the United States at the beginning of the 20th Century enjoyed everything life could offer. And they were making life better for others at the same time. Hispanic contribution to American science, industry, art, education and politics became legendary during this time.

The 1900s also were a time of great scientific learning. Many of the inventions and discoveries we take for granted today were the result of hard work by Hispanics.

Juan Guiteras helped discover how the human body fights diseases. Guiteras was an American doctor who wondered why some children in jungle villages became sick with yellow fever while others did not. His experiments later showed that people could become immune to certain diseases by being injected with very low doses of the viruses that cause those diseases. This discovery paved the way for other doctors to develop special medicines that prevent all kinds of terrible sicknesses. Guiteras was born in Cuba but later moved to the United States. He graduated from the University of Pennsylvania. After medical school, he worked in hospitals and taught at colleges.

Carlos Finlay was another Hispanic doctor interested in solving the problem of yellow fever. Finlay knew it was caused by a virus. He thought that if he could learn how people caught yellow fever there might be a way to stop it. Finlay's research soon uncovered the mystery. It was mosquitos. He discovered that somehow mosquitos carried the disease from one person to another. Get rid of the mosquitos and the disease will go away, too, he said. And he was right.

And then there was Oswaldo Cruz. Cruz was a Brazilian doctor who discovered a cure for another terrible disease that had killed many people all over the world. That disease was smallpox.

In 1903, two Anglos by the name of Orville and Wilbur Wright launched a new age by being the first to build and fly a powered airplane. But much

Carlos Finlay, a Hispanic doctor, discovered that mosquitos spread yellow fever.

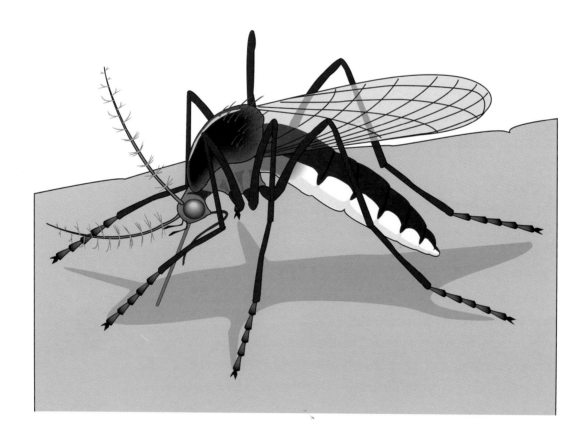

of what they knew about flight came from Carlos Antonio Obregon. Obregon was a famous builder and flyer of gliders. Gliders are airplanes that fly without the help of an engine.

It wasn't long before airplanes began filling the skies. One famous early pilot was Horacio Ruiz. He flew the world's first airmail route in 1917.

The early 20th Century was a great time for inventions big and small. In 1911, Alfonso Alvarez invented the first safety razor so people could shave themselves without getting cut. One year later, Pedro Fernandez invented the adjustable wrench.

Also in 1912, Elena de Valdez became the first woman in the United States to patent an invention. To patent something means no one can copy your invention without paying you for your permission.

Bird-watching became a favorite hobby for many people at the beginning of the 20th Century. Among the best-loved bird illustrators was Louis Agassiz Fuertes. Fuertes was a native of Upstate New York and the son of a man who was dean of the civil engineering school at Cornell University. In 1898 Fuertes began drawing pictures of birds. He traveled to Alaska in 1899 as a part of the Harriman Expedition that explored the unknown wilderness in that giant state.

He later traveled throughout the Southwest and then down into Central and South America where he drew pictures of all the many birds there. He had a photographic memory, so he was able to remember perfectly every tiny detail about each bird he saw.

5
THE FIRST
WORLD WAR

The entire world went to war in 1914. Germany tried to take over France and Britain. The United States managed to stay out of the war for three years. Finally, in 1917, the United States came to the rescue of France and Britain. The war lasted until 1918. It became known as the First World War.

Many frightening new weapons were used during the war. Among these were the tank, the submarine and the airplane. The first person to pilot an airplane in war was an Hispanic by the name of Gustavo Salinas. The year was 1914.

Before the war ended in 1918, many Hispanics were wrongly accused of wanting Germany to win. Anglos thought this was so because Mexico had been friendly with Germany before the war and because many German families had settled in Mexico. The truth is that Hispanics fought bravely against Germany as soldiers and sailors in the United States military.

Many Hispanics fought bravely against Germany during World War I.

6
THE ROARING TWENTIES

The 1920s was a time of great prosperity in America. People who had very little money became wealthy almost overnight by investing their savings in the stock market. Even Hispanics were enjoying the fruits of a growing economy. Hispanics with money became very interested in establishing newspapers of their own. And there was a new invention called radio. Hispanics wanted radio stations of their own, too.

But the good times came to a halt in 1929. People suddenly lost confidence in the stock market that had made all the prosperity possible. There was panic. People tried to sell their stocks. But there were no buyers. In a matter of days, stocks that once were worth millions of dollars weren't even worth a penny.

The factories were forced to close because too few people were left with money to buy the things the factories made. That meant the factories had to stop making things. And without things to make, the factory owners had no need of workers. Many workers were fired from their jobs. The fired workers couldn't pay the rent on their homes and were forced to live in the streets. People couldn't even afford to buy much food. For the next 10 years there was great sorrow in the land. This time was known as the Great Depression.

7
SURVIVING THE GREAT DEPRESSION

The Great Depression of the 1930s caused many farmers to go out of business. Among them were Hispanics who had owned farms that had been theirs for generations. They lost these farms because they did not have enough money to pay their taxes. So, the government took the farms away from them and sold the land to anyone who had the cash. Usually, the farms were sold for only a small part of their actual worth.

Those Hispanics and Anglos who did not lose their farms discovered there were fewer and fewer buyers for the crops they grew. Farming slowed way down as a result, and that meant not as many people were needed to work in the fields. No work meant that many of the Hispanic farm workers who came from Mexico were forced to return there.

The Great Depression was bad, but Ameri-

During the Depression, many lost their jobs and had to stand in food lines to survive.

cans found ways to keep smiling. Many sought escape from their problems by going to the movies. Hispanics played a big role in Hollywood. In fact, the Hollywood film industry today would be much different were it not for Hispanics.

The first motion picture camera used in the United States was invented by an Hispanic in 1895. That person was Thomas Alva Edison who also invented the electric light bulb and the phonograph. Other types of movie cameras were invented by Hispanics in Central and South America about the same time Edison invented his.

The first real superstar of American movies was an Hispanic. His name was Ramon Novarro. He was very popular in the 1920s. Novarro starred in many films, but perhaps his best was the original "Ben-Hur" in which he raced thundering Roman chariots and survived a flaming-arrow battle at sea between ancient warships.

Thomas Alva Edison with his invention, the phonograph.

Movies had no sound when they first were made at the beginning of the century. The only way the audience knew what was being said was when the words were shown on the screen between scenes. That changed in 1927 when the first film with sound was produced. It was called a "talkie"

and it was made in America. But the equipment needed to make such a movie was invented by Hispanics in 1919.

Everyone seemed to love the movies. But there was an invention developed during the 1930s that people would later love even more. It was the television. Guillermo Gonzalez Camarena was an engineer who used his knowledge of mathematics to help invent the very first color television.

Movie star Ramon Novarro in "Ben Hur."

8
THE COMING
OF WAR

America came out of the Great Depression as World War II drew near. By 1939, Europe was again a battleground as Adolf Hitler's Nazi Germany tried to conquer the world. German forces conquered France in 1940 and came close to defeating Britain and the Soviet Union. Germany's friend in the war was Japan. Japan conquered much of China and parts of Asia. The German and Japanese victories caused the British, the Soviets and the Chinese to turn to America for help. The United States wanted to stay out of the war. But President Franklin D. Roosevelt agreed to send thousands of airplanes, tanks, ships and supplies.

American factories produced the weapons of war the allies of America needed to fight Germany and Japan. Now the factories hummed with activity. Jobs that had been hard to find during the Great Depression suddenly were available. The United States went back to work in a big way. People again were able to buy more food and farmers worked harder than ever to keep up with the demand.

The United States asked Mexico to send back the farm workers who had been forced to leave during the Great Depression. But Mexico said no. The United States begged. But Mexico would not agree unless the United States promised to give housing and medicine to the farm workers. Finally, the

United States gave in and said it would do so. About 250,000 Mexicans worked on U.S. farms between 1942 and 1947. In 1947, the United States said it no longer would take care of these workers.

The farm workers borrowed from Mexico were called "braceros." That is slang for hired hand. They worked in the fields of the Southwest six months of each year. They planted the seeds, took care of the young crops and then harvested what had grown. They worked very long and very hard but received very little money for their labors. However, it was much more money than they could have earned doing the same work in Mexico. For that reason many Mexicans wanted to be braceros. It didn't matter that they would be forced to sleep in chicken coops. It didn't matter that there would be no doctors to treat their illnesses. All that mattered was the chance to work and make money.

Farmers knew this. And many of them were bad to the braceros. They were bad even though they knew that without the braceros' help their farms would suffer greatly. The braceros were easy victims because they usually could not read or write their native language of Spanish and certainly could not speak English. Nor did they understand the U.S. laws. And because of these disadvantages, they never really knew where to turn for help.

9
THE UNITED STATES ENTERS THE WAR

The United States went to war in 1941 after Japan bombed the American Navy base at Pearl Harbor, Hawaii. The government issued a call for men all over the country to join the Army, Navy or Marines. Hispanics answered that call by signing up in record numbers. A great many of them returned home after the war ended in 1945 as highly decorated heroes.

Meanwhile, the United States was racing to develop superweapons. The military leaders had learned that Germany was secretly trying to be the first to build an atomic bomb, just one of which could destroy an entire city. The United States knew it would lose the war if Germany succeeded with its plan to build the atomic bomb. So the United States set out to build atomic bombs of its own and beat Germany at its own game. The United States brought all its brainiest scientists together in a super-secret effort called the Manhattan Project. America was depending on these scientists for its very survival. One of the geniuses who played an important role in building the first atomic bomb was an Hispanic-American by the name of Luis Alvarez (1911-1988). Alvarez was a physicist who understood the mysteries of atoms and the tremendous power locked away inside them.

Alvarez also helped invent a type of radar to safely guide airplanes in for a landing through thick clouds. In 1968, he won the Nobel prize for his lifetime of work in attempting to solve complicated physics problems. And Alvarez later was one of the very first scientists to theorize that dinosaurs became extinct because of a comet or meteor impact. (The meteor or comet threw enough dust into the air to block off the sun's light, killing the plants that dinosaurs ate.)

Germany surrendered before it could complete an atomic bomb. But Japan continued to fight. The United States dropped two atomic bombs on Japan in August 1945. The bombs were so unbelievably destructive that Japan surrendered a few days later. World War II was over.

Nobel prize winning physicist Luis Alvarez.

10
HISPANICS AND POST–WAR AMERICA

Hispanics returned home from the war to a United States that was becoming more and more wealthy. The decade of the 1950s was a time when people lived better and more comfortably than ever before.

But there were threats to this way of life. Some countries that were America's friends soon became enemies. China was one of them. The Soviet Union was another. Both countries had come to possess atomic bombs and worse. People in the United States worried that the Soviets or the Chinese would attack with their many nuclear weapons. Never before had there been such a frightening threat to world peace. Humanity now stood for the very first time at the brink of total self-destruction.

Americans once again found ways to forget their troubles. Many of them got caught up in the dance craze of the mambo. Mambo has a fast beat and lots of drums. It was invented in Cuba. People could enjoy the mambo at a dance club or by listening to it on phonograph records. In 1954, Manuel Perusquia was the first to figure out a way to record and play music in stereo.

Other Americans stayed home and watched television. Televisions first became widely used in homes during this period. One person who helped make the TV industry what it is today was Desi

Arnaz. He was born in Cuba in 1917 and was from a wealthy family. He came to America in the 1930s to play drums in a famous band. Then, he became a comedy actor. He married comedienne Lucille Ball. Together they starred in several movies. In 1950, they began their own TV company and called it Desilu Productions. The television program for which Arnaz is most famous is "I Love Lucy." He played Ricky Ricardo. Up until then, all television shows were broadcast live. The actors would stand in front of a single camera and recite their lines. If they made a mistake, the whole world saw it. But Arnaz came up with the idea of filming the shows first and then broadcasting them. That way, if anything went wrong, the mistake could be re-shot before it was shown on TV. No one at home would see the mistake. He also had the idea of setting up a camera at each side of the stage and one in front to make sure the audience wouldn't get bored from always looking at the show from just one angle. Today, all TV comedy shows are done this way.

Another favorite pastime of Americans during the 1950s was baseball. A player people loved greatly was Roberto Clemente. He was born in Puerto Rico in 1934. It wasn't long before people everywhere realized Clemente was among the most gifted players in history.

Desi Arnaz with wife Lucy. On the "I Love Lucy" show, he played Lucy's husband Ricky Ricardo.

The Dodgers hired him in 1954. Back then, the Dodgers still made their home in Brooklyn, New York, not Los Angeles, California. But in those days, major league baseball players were almost always Anglos. There were only a few African-Americans and no Hispanics. Because of that the Dodgers decided to place Clemente on their minor league

farm team in Montreal for that first season. It was while he was playing for Montreal that the Pittsburgh Pirates saw him and asked him to join their team. He did. The Pirates were very fortunate to have Clemente playing for them. They had been the last-place team for many seasons. That all changed when Clemente came aboard. Before they knew it, the Pirates had become World Series champions. And Clemente won four National League batting titles. Clemente was one of a handfull of players in baseball history to get 3,000 lifetime hits.

Roberto Clemente died in 1972 when the jetliner he was traveling on crashed at sea. Clemente was on his way to bring emergency food, water and clothing to victims of an earthquake that destroyed much of Managua, Nicaragua, only a few days earlier.

Pittsburgh Pirates slugger Roberto Clemente won four batting titles.

11
THE UNDOCUMENTED WORKER PROBLEM

\The farms of the United States produced more food than ever thanks to new ways of raising crops. That meant more work for the braceros. In 1948, the government agreed to start the bracero program again. This second program lasted 16 years. This time, nearly 5 million foreign Hispanics took part in it. But many others became braceros without taking part in the official program. There were too many papers to fill out and too many questions to answer. It seemed so much easier to cross the border from Mexico into the United States without official permission. And so there began a steadily growing flow of workers from Mexico and other Latin American countries who broke the law in order to reach this land of opportunity.

The farmers liked the undocumented workers because they could pay them much less than the braceros. The undocumented workers could not complain. They knew they would be arrested and sent back to Mexico the minute they complained about the farmers. They were trapped.

Many undocumented workers gave up on the farms and found jobs in the cities. But many factory owners were just like the farmers. They paid very little money and felt they could get away with doing so because the undocumented workers would not complain to the authorities.

12
TROUBLE IN CUBA

The Platt Amendment of 1903 gave the United States permission to build a Navy base at Guantanamo Bay in Cuba. It also opened the door for American businesses to set up operations on the island. For many years the United States enjoyed good relations with Cuba. Those good relations were helped along by the Cuban government. But in 1933, Fulgencio Batista y Zaldivar took over the government. He was a dictator who allowed the people of Cuba to suffer just as they had when the island was ruled by Spain. Things were so bad that a man by the name of Fidel Castro decided to lead a revolution against Batista in 1956. The fighting went on for three years. Finally, Castro won.

Castro's victory caused many Cubans to flee to the United States. They did not like Castro because he believed that Cubans should give to his government everything they owned. Such a system of government is called communism. It was the same system as in the Soviet Union and China.

Many of those who left Cuba settled in Miami, Florida. They worked very hard to build a strong community of their own where they and their children could be free to do great things with their lives. And they succeeded. Miami became a more wonderful city because of the contributions made by its Cuban community.

Castro at first tried to be friendly with the United States. But the American government could not support a communist dictator like Castro. The United States and Castro's Cuba became enemies. Castro then turned to the Soviet Union for help. The Soviet Union was only too happy to send food, clothes and money.

The Soviets sent to Cuba one thing more: nuclear missiles for a possible attack against United States. In the early 1960s, the Soviet Union began building on Cuba bases from which these missiles could be launched. The missiles would be able to swiftly carry nuclear warheads straight into the heart of the United States. America would have little time to defend itself.

President John F. Kennedy told the Soviet Union to remove its missiles from Cuba. The Soviet Union said no. Kennedy warned that the United States would fire nuclear missiles of its own at the Soviet Union unless the Cuban missiles were removed. The Soviet Union continued to say no. For several days in October of 1962 it looked as if another world war was about to begin. America and the Soviet Union pointed their nuclear weapons at one another. Everyone held their breath. This would be a war like no other in history. Hundreds of millions of people in the warring countries could perish in a matter of hours. Life on Planet Earth itself could come to an end.

Fortunately, the Soviet Union backed down at the last possible minute. All-out nuclear war was

Cuban refugees brave the Gulf of Mexico in their tiny raft, hoping for freedom in the United States.

27

avoided. And the Soviet missiles were removed from Cuba.

But Castro continued for many years afterward to be a thorn in the side of the United States. In 1980, Castro allowed tens of thousands of Cubans to leave the island for the United States. Their arrival was a hardship on the American government because it had to shelter, feed and clothe all those people. Many of those whom Castro had sent to the United States were actually hardened criminals that soon began bringing terror to the streets of cities all across America. In 1994, Castro again allowed Cubans by the tens of thousands to leave. But, this time, the United States sent them back to Cuba.

13
EPILOGUE

There never was a nation as blessed as America during the post-war years. Not even the prosperity in the years before the Great Depression came close to matching it.

Many Hispanics shared in the wealth of America. However, there were many more who received only a few crumbs. Those who did not prosper began to demand their fair share of the opportunities. But they would have to wait for the arrival of the civil rights movement.

GLOSSARY

ANGLOS
People of the Caucasian or white race.

ATOMIC BOMB
A weapon that causes vast destruction by releasing the energy contained in atoms. Atoms are the tiniest units of matter known to exist.

CULTURE
The arts, sciences and life style of a nation's people.

DISCRIMINATION
Unfair treatment by one person or group against another individual or group.

IMMIGRANTS
People who come from one country to take up permanent residence in another.

INDUSTRIALIZATION
To have a growing number of machines doing work that previously could be performed only by hand.

NOBEL PRIZE
A prize given once a year to people who help humanity through their work in science, the arts or peacemaking.

NUCLEAR WEAPONS
Any explosive that uses atomic energy. See "atomic bomb."

PHONOGRAPH
A device for playing recorded music or speech.

PHYSICIST
A special kind of scientist who tries to unlock the secrets of matter and energy.

SATELLITE
A container full of electronic equipment and cameras that orbits the Earth and sends useful pictures or information down to a tracking station on the ground.

STOCK MARKET
A place where people can buy or sell ownership in a vast number of different companies. Such companies raise money to pay for things they need by offering the public one or more shares of ownership, or stock. The price a person pays to buy each share of stock depends on how well the company is doing.

UNDOCUMENTED WORKER
An immigrant who breaks the law by sneaking into the United States and then applies for a job. Immigrants who enter by legal means receive papers, or documents, to prove they have received government permission to live and work here. Those who sneak in receive no such documents and are then said to be undocumented. It is against the law for businesses to hire undocumented workers.

UNION
A group of workers who have banded together to act as one when demanding better pay from their employer. A union can greatly damage a company when all the members decide not to work. This is called striking. A strike usually ends when the company owners suffer enough economic loss and decide to agree to the demands of the union.

BIBLIOGRAPHY

Lepthien, Emilie U. *The Philippines*, 1984, Children's Press, Chicago, IL.

Loza, Steven. *Barrio Rhythm.* 1993, University of Illinois Press, Urbana, IL.

Martinez, Rueben. "Shock of the New." Article in Los Angeles Times Magazine, January 30, 1994.

Ross, Fred. *Conquering Goliath.* 1989, El Taller Grafico, Keene, CA.

Sinnott, Susan. *Extraordinary Hispanic Americans.* 1991, Children's Press, Chicago.

Various contributors. *World Book Encyclopedia.* Field Enterprises, Chicago.

Various contributors. *Encyclopaedia Brittanica.* Encyclopaedia Brittanica Inc., London and Chicago.

INDEX